THE HOLOCAUST
AFTER THE HOLOCAUST

Sean Sheehan

RAINTREE
STECK-VAUGHN
PUBLISHERS

A Harcourt Company

Austin   New York
www.raintreesteckvaughn.com

Titles in the series: Causes • The Death Camps •
Survival and Resistance • After the Holocaust

Published by Raintree Steck-Vaughn Publishers,
an imprint of Steck-Vaughn Company

Library of Congress Cataloging-in-Publication Data

Sheehan, Sean, 1951-
    After the Holocaust / Sean Sheehan.
        p. cm. -- (Holocaust)
    Includes bibliographical references (p .) and index.
    ISBN 0-7398-3259-X
    1. Holocaust, Jewish (1939–1945)--Influence--Juvenile literature.
2 Holocaust, Jewish (1939-1945)--Moral and ethical aspects--Juvenile
literature. 3. Jews--History--1945--Juvenile literature. [1. Holocaust,
Jewish (1939-1945) 2. Jews--History--1945. 3. Holocaust survivors.]
I. Title. II. Holocaust (Austin, Tex.)

D804.34 .S52 2001
909'.04924--dc21   00-045752

Printed in Italy. Bound in the United States.
1 2 3 4 5 6 7 8 9 0 06 05 04 03 02

*Cover photos: The perimeter
fence at Auschwitz
concentration camp in Poland;
girl grieving at an Auschwitz
crematorium*

*Page 1: Memorial window for
the Holocaust Survivors Centre,
Hendon, London, by Moshe
Galili*

Acknowledgments

AKG London: pages 7b, 8, 9, 12,
16l, 16r, 17t, 18t, 18b, 20, 22,
26t, 30, 32l, 40, 50t, 59r; Camera
Press: cover (background photo),
pages 4, 6, 28, 41; Hulton-Getty
Picture Collection: pages 13t, 13b,
21, 38t, 38b, 53; Eye Ubiquitous:
page 54b (copyright Leon
Schadeberg); Moshe Galili: pages 1
and 44t; Ronald Grant Archive:
pages 15b, 44b, 45, 46, 47t;
Imperial War Museum: pages 39t,
39b; PA News: page 34b; Panos
Pictures: page 55t (copyright John
Spaull), page 55b (copyright J.C.
Tordai); Popperfoto: pages 15t, 17b,
23t, 23b, 24, 25, 26b, 27, 29, 31t,
31b, 32r, 33, 34t/35t, 35b, 36,
42t, 42b, 43, 47b, 48, 49, 54t, 56,
57; Chris Schwarz: cover (main
photo), pages 5, 50b, 51, 58, 59l;
US Holocaust Memorial Museum:
pages 7t, 10, 11, 14, 19, 52. The
map on page 5 is adapted from a
map in Martin Gilbert, *The Dent
Atlas of Jewish History* (copyright
Martin Gilbert).

CONTENTS

A NEW LIFE?

THE HOLOCAUST was an act of genocide carried out by Nazi Germany that took the lives of more than 6 million Jews. The precise number of victims is not known, but most of them died between 1939 and 1945, during World War II. What makes the Holocaust different from other acts of genocide is not the number of people who died, nor the act itself, but the manner in which it was conceived and carried out. There have been other periods in history, before and since, when ethnic and religious groups have been persecuted and murdered in large numbers. But the Nazis planned the Holocaust, using industrial technology to build large-scale death camps and efficiently organizing the transportation and slaughter of Jews from every corner of German-occupied Europe.

It was only the military defeat of Germany in World War II that brought the Holocaust to an end. If Germany had not been defeated, the Nazi plan to murder every European Jew would have been carried

Below: Victims of the Einsatzgruppen were mostly buried in large pits, but the death camps had their own crematoriums, where incinerators—like this one from Bergen-Belsen camp—were used to burn the bodies.

Holocaust Language

Holocaust term used since the World War II to refer to the systematic murder of more than six million Jews by German Nazis. The word, which comes from the Greek translation of an Old Testament word, means "a sacrifice that is completely consumed by fire."

death camps also known as extermination camps, death camps were designed to systematically murder their inmates, mostly Jews. The Nazi death camps were in Poland: Auschwitz, Belzec, Chelmno, Majdanek, Sobibor, and Treblinka.

Einsatzgruppen a special task force of the German army that sought out and murdered Jews, communists, and other people regarded as enemies of the Nazi state.

genocide the deliberate and systematic destruction of a national, racial, religious, political, or ethnic group. The term was first used by an international lawyer to describe the Nazi murder of European Jews.

Shoah the Hebrew word for the Holocaust.

through. While they were in operation, the death camps were devastatingly effective. At the Treblinka death camp, for example, 99 out of every 100 Jews who arrived there had been gassed within hours of their train's arrival at the camp station. Special death squads operating in eastern Europe, known as *Einsatzgruppen*, had already killed as many Jews as would die in the death camps. By the time the war came to an end more than six million Jews had fallen victim to the Holocaust. More than half the Jewish population of Europe, one-third of all the Jews in the world, was dead.

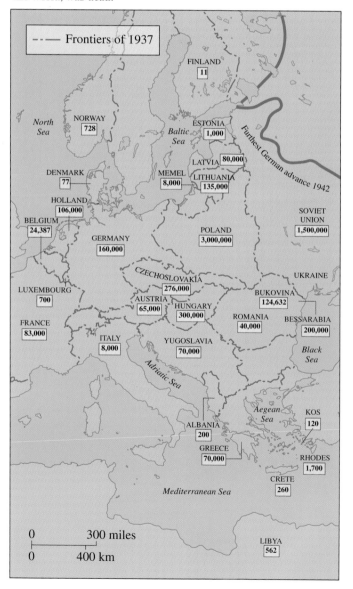

Above: The ashes collected from the Auschwitz incinerators were dumped in this field, close to the death camp in Poland. At the height of the Holocaust the crematoriums were operating 24 hours a day.

Left: Historian Martin Gilbert's estimates of Jews murdered in Europe between September 1, 1939 and May 8, 1945.

The Death Camps

The six specially built death camps (those using gas for the systematic extermination of Jews and other prisoners) were situated in eastern Poland. By the end of 1944, when Soviet troops were advancing across Poland toward Berlin, some of them had been closed down and their equipment had been destroyed. This was not the case at Majdanek, which the Soviet soldiers reached first. German prisoners were forced to take a tour of the camp. Western journalists were also invited to see the camp and the first stories of the Holocaust began appearing in Europe and the United States. Auschwitz, the largest and most sophisticated of the death camps, was liberated on January 27, 1945, by Soviet soldiers. By then most of the remaining prisoners had already been forced out by their guards and marched at gunpoint to camps in Germany.

The concentration camps in western Germany were liberated by American and British troops beginning in April 1945. The troops were horrified when they saw the survivors of the camp, most of whom were emaciated and barely alive. Many had also endured the forced marches from camps in Poland. Germany's camps had become grossly overcrowded with the survivors of forced marches from Auschwitz and labor camps in the east. Now the barbarous treatment the Jews had undergone became known to the world.

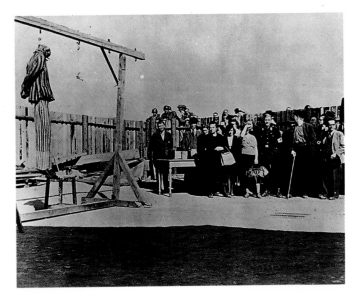

Left: After the liberation of Buchenwald concentration camp in Germany in 1945, citizens from the nearby town of Weimar were forced to confront some of the atrocities that had taken place there. Here, they are shown the body of a victim hanging in the camp's yard.

One of the worst-affected camps was Bergen-Belsen. Many of the prisoners there were too weak to survive, and thousands died in the weeks after liberation. Those victims who did manage to survive the war still found themselves under guard in camps surrounded by barbed wire. At Dachau, the survivors were told that anyone found outside the camp without a permit would be shot.

Continuing Anti-Semitism

Europe was in chaos after the war. Millions of people, officially described as displaced persons (DPs), were moving back and forth across Europe, trying to return to their homes and communities. In Germany alone there were some 9 million displaced persons. Special DP camps were established across Europe and even in the United States. Many Holocaust survivors, wondering how they would start their lives once more, lived in these camps in the first years after the war. Sometimes these camps also housed German soldiers and Nazi collaborators as prisoners. Little thought was given as to how Jewish refugees might feel about this.

Above: Prisoners are forced to march from Dachau. As Allied troops approached the camps, the Nazis led the surviving prisoners on forced marches, hoping to use them as laborers somewhere else. Because of the likelihood that the harsh pace would kill many of the already weakened prisoners, and the certainty that anyone who could not keep up would be shot, they were known as death marches.

Left: This photograph, taken at Bergen-Belsen in April 1945, shows Allied troops supervising the removal of corpses from the camp. "Every other day," a soldier wrote home to his wife, "the bodies are collected and buried and there is always an open grave."

Approximately 1 million Jews survived in countries that had once been ruled by the Nazis. Many of these also became displaced persons. At first, many Jews returned to where they had once lived, but their homes and culture in eastern Europe had been virtually destroyed and could never be truly restored. Their property had been destroyed or given to others, and many survivors returned to find that they were the only members of their family who were still alive. Many began to look to the West instead. Over time, the center of Jewish civilization shifted from Eastern Europe to the United States.

Another problem confronting Jews was the legacy of anti-Semitism. The traditional prejudice against Jews had been developed by the Nazis into an ideology (organized belief system). Throughout the 1930s, the Nazi Party had fueled anti-Semitic attitudes that had existed in Europe for centuries before Adolf Hitler came to power. The German government had encouraged the idea that Jews were *Untermenschen* ("subhumans"). When the war came to an end in 1945, anti-Semitic prejudice did not simply disappear from Europe.

Left: A Soviet vehicle passes through the remnants of a village on its way to Berlin in March 1945. Holocaust survivors had to return to ruined villages like this.

Surviving the War

Between 100,000 and 200,000 Jews survived the death squads, the ghettos, the concentration camps and the death marches, but they did not all survive the legacy of anti-Semitism. Even in the liberated camp of Dachau, in May 1945, there were protests by non-Jewish Polish prisoners against the holding of a Jewish religious service in the main square of the camp. And, at one DP camp, Poles destroyed the Jewish prayer house. Eventually, DP camps solely for Jews were established, but these were often overcrowded and unhygienic.

Left: Survivors celebrate the liberation of Dachau in April 1945

We Do Not Want Revenge

Zalman Grinberg, a Jewish doctor who survived life in a ghetto and death marches, delivered these words to fellow survivors at Dachau concentration camp in May 1945:
Hitler has lost every battle on every front except the battle against defenseless and unarmed men, women, and children. He won the war against the Jews of Europe. He carried out this war with the help of the German nation.

However, we do not want revenge. If we took this vengeance it would mean we would fall to the depths of ethics and morals the German nation has been in these past ten years.

We are not able to slaughter women and children! We are not able to burn millions of people! We are not able to starve hundreds of thousands.

(Quoted in Martin Gilbert, *The Holocaust: The Jewish Tragedy*)

Demoralized Beyond Hope

Some of the problems faced by Holocaust survivors in the DP camps and elsewhere were shared by other Europeans: food shortages, inadequate housing, and no organized employment. What could not be shared with others was the survivor's state of mind. After years of systematic cruelty and persecution, with most of their families wiped out, facing the future was no easy task for Jewish survivors. One journalist described the atmosphere in Jewish camps as "one of apathy, grayness, and despair." The people of one DP camp "appeared demoralized beyond hope of rehabilitation. They appear to be beaten both spiritually and physically, with no hopes or incentives for the future." This was hardly surprising, in view of what they had experienced.

Below: The first group of displaced persons arrives at the Zeilsheim DP camp in Germany

Thousands of Jews were murdered in eastern Europe in the months after the end of the war, including many who had survived life in Auschwitz, Treblinka, and other camps. More than 1,000 Jews were killed in Poland between 1945 and 1947, a higher number than in the whole decade before the outbreak of the war. 40 Jews were killed in an outbreak of anti-Semitism in the Polish town of Kielce in 1946. This confirmed the fears of many surviving Jews in eastern Europe. Around 100,000 Jews fled Eastern Europe and sought a new life in western Europe, Palestine, or the United States.

Ironically, for many of those fleeing Jews, Germany became a temporary place of refuge. In 1945, the number of Jewish DPs in the American-occupied zone of Germany increased from 40,000 to nearly 150,000, mostly from Poland. Many of them had their sights set on a new life in Palestine, where demands were growing for an independent state for the Jewish people. It was not going to be possible to rebuild the Jewish civilization that had flourished in eastern Europe before the onslaught of Nazism.

Above: This official photograph of a street scene at a DP camp in Germany gives no hint of the terrible distress experienced by those trying to rebuild their shattered lives.

THE BIRTH OF ISRAEL

T HE ZIONIST movement, based on the idea that Jews should establish their own political state in their biblical homeland of Palestine, developed toward the end of the 19th century. The movement took its name from one of the hills of Jerusalem, Zion, which came to represent the cultural and political homeland of Jews. Jerusalem was then part of Palestine, which in turn was part of the Turkish empire. Early Zionists wanted to buy land belonging to the Turkish authorities and settle in Palestine.

The region known as Palestine is sacred to Jews, Christians, and Muslims, and for centuries its territory has been claimed by different religious, national, and ethnic groups. Also known as the Holy Land, and as Judea, the ancient land of the Jews, its Jewish population increased fivefold during the 1920s and 1930s, but Arabs still made up 70 percent of the total population.

Opposite top: British troops march into Jerusalem at the end of World War I in 1918.

Opposite below: The head of the British Zionist movement, Lionel Walter Rothschild (far right), meets with the Jewish scientist Albert Einstein.

Below: Arthur Balfour was Great Britain's foreign secretary from 1916 to 1919.

The British Mandate

With the collapse of the Ottoman Empire after World War I, Great Britain took control of Palestine. During the war, the British government had made promises to both Jewish and Arab groups about the future of Palestine. They promised independence for Arabs in the Middle East, but they also promised "a national home for the Jewish people." In both cases, the British wanted support for their own economic and political interests in the Middle East once the Ottoman Empire was broken up. After the war, the League of Nations, an international peacekeeping organization, awarded control of Palestine to Great Britain.

The Balfour Declaration

In November 1917, Arthur Balfour, the British foreign secretary, wrote to Lord Lionel Rothschild, head of the British Zionist movement, expressing Britain's sympathy with the Zionists' aims:

His Majesty's Government view with favour the establishment in Palestine of a national home for the Jewish people and will use their best endeavours to facilitate the achievement of this object, it being clearly understood that nothing shall be done that may prejudice the civil and religious rights of existing non-Jewish communities in Palestine or the rights and political status enjoyed by Jews in other countries.

Zionism in the 1940s

In 1939, when war with Germany was very likely, Great Britain wanted to stay on friendly terms with the Arabs to keep them from becoming allies of Hitler. Great Britain therefore set severe limits on the number of Jews allowed to settle in Palestine. This could not have happened at a worse time for Jews in Europe. To make matters worse, the Zionists in Palestine failed to come to the aid of Europe's Jews. Until 1941 (when the Jews were no longer allowed to emigrate from Nazi-occupied Europe), Zionists did little to help those who were trying to flee. Nor was much done by the Zionist movement during the war itself. When the war came to an end in 1945, the British were still severely restricting emigration to Palestine. But now there were many thousands of Jewish refugees looking for somewhere to live.

After the war, Jewish underground forces in Palestine, the Irgun and Stern Gang, organized armed resistance against the British to support the creation of an independent state. Acts of terrorism in Palestine caused the deaths of civilians and soldiers, which led to anti-Semitic riots in Great Britain and the defacing of synagogues. Jewish refugees arrived in Palestine as illegal immigrants in ships, only to be arrested by British troops. One boat carrying refugees who wanted to settle in Palestine carried a banner with these words: "We survived Hitler. Death is no stranger to us. Nothing can keep us from our Jewish homeland. The blood be on your head if you fire on this unarmed ship."

Such events gained public support for the plight of Jews, and the United States pressured Great Britain to change its policy in Palestine. In 1947, when the *Exodus*, a ship carrying Jewish illegal immigrants, was fired on by the British and people were killed, the plight of refugees became a matter of international concern. The problem for the British was that the Zionist demand for an independent state caused conflict with the Arabs who had lived in Palestine. By the time of the *Exodus* incident,

Opposite top: The lower deck of the Exodus shows the damage received in its encounter with British forces, who were ordered not to let it land its cargo of illegal Jewish immigrants in Palestine.

Below: During World War II British Jews gather outside an office in London's East End where a petition is being drawn up to ease immigration of Jewish refugees into Palestine.

The *Exodus*

In 1947, a ship from the south of France, the *Exodus*, arrived off the coast of Palestine carrying 4,500 Jewish survivors of the Holocaust. When British troops tried to board the ship, there was resistance from the refugees, and the British used machine guns to gain control. Three people were killed; many more were injured. The British then forced the ship to take the refugees to Germany. The spectacle of survivors being forced to return to the country that had been the cause of their terrible suffering in the first place increased public support for the Zionist cause.

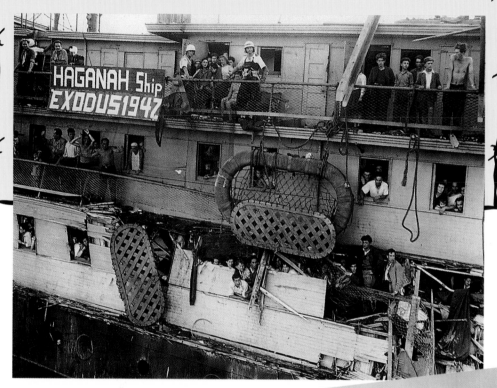

Great Britain had for centuries given up trying to resolve the situation. In February 1947 Britain declared that the United Nations should deal with the problem and that British troops would leave Palestine on May 15, 1948.

Right: Paul Newman starred in the film Exodus, *which dramatized the events of the tragic journey of the ship of that name in 1947.*

The Creation of Israel

In November 1947, the United Nations passed a resolution proposing that Palestine be divided into separate states, Arab and Jewish. The city of Jerusalem would belong to neither state and would be under United Nations control. The resolution did not please the Arab inhabitants, who objected to the fact that more than half of their homeland would now be given to a Jewish community. At the time, the Jewish community made up one-third of the total population and owned one-eighth of the land of Palestine.

On the day before the British departed, at 4 P.M. on May 14, 1948, the state of Israel was declared in the city of Tel Aviv. The next day, the neighboring Arab countries of Egypt, Syria, Lebanon, Iraq, and Transjordan (now Jordan) launched an attack on Israel. The first Arab-Israeli war had begun. There were more Arab-Israeli wars to come, resulting in Israel occupying large areas of land that had long been under Arab control. The occupation of Arab territory by Israel remains a controversial topic and an obstacle to peace in the Middle East.

Israel and the Holocaust

The Zionist movement, which gave birth to demands for a Jewish state in Palestine, existed long before the Holocaust. Early

The declaration of the birth of Israel in May 1948 (below right) brought a swift response from the majority Arab population of Palestine and led to Arab freedom fighters forming their own army (below left). The Arab-Israeli conflict of today has its origins in the creation of the independent nation of Israel.

Left: In the first months of Israel's existence barricades were erected in Jerusalem, separating the Arab and Jewish quarters of the city.

Zionism, at the beginning of the 20th century, was a response to the longstanding European anti-Semitism, particularly in Poland and Russia. It was the unleashing of anti-Semitism by the Nazis and its revival in eastern Europe that fueled the development of Zionism in the 1930s. Large minorities of Jews in eastern Europe had suffered persecution under governments that were happy to exploit anti-Semitic feelings. When Hitler gained power in Germany, and extended his rule to Austria, Czechoslovakia, Poland, and the Baltic states (Lithuania, Latvia, and Estonia), he was able to make use of governments and political groups that shared the Nazi prejudice against Jews.

Above: Another march of Jews, this time to new homes in Israel. The newly created state of Israel symbolized the hopes of the Jews as a people, while to the Arabs it remained an unacceptable situation forced upon them.

After the war, the search by Holocaust survivors for a new home, and their pressing moral claim for special treatment, strengthened the call for a Jewish state in Palestine. It is also true that many countries looked favorably on the idea of a new Jewish state because it removed the problem of trying to accommodate large numbers of refugees in their own lands.

In the second half of 1945, some 90,000 Jewish refugees went to Palestine from parts of Europe that had been occupied by the Nazis. Over the next three years, another 60,000 arrived, and in 1948, the year when Israel became an independent state, the numbers swelled to nearly 200,000. By the end of 1949, almost one out of every three Israelis was a survivor from Nazi Europe.

SEEKING JUSTICE

T HE IDEA that people could find themselves in court for crimes committed in the course of a war existed long before World War II. In 1945, however, it was felt that special charges should be brought against some of the leaders held responsible for starting the war and taking it to new levels of brutality. This new concept of war crimes included conventional crimes that soldiers could be held responsible for, like the shooting of an unarmed prisoner or civilian, but also included two more charges. One was"crimes against peace," for launching a war of aggression, and another was "crimes against humanity," for persecuting a particular group on the grounds of race, religion, or politics. These charges could be used to prosecute people who may never have worn a uniform but who, while sitting safely behind a desk, organized acts of genocide. Hitler himself had escaped justice by committing suicide in April 1945.

The governments of the United States, Great Britain, and the Soviet Union—had declared in 1943 that they would seek to punish their enemies for war crimes, and preparations went ahead for this in 1945. There was some disagreement, with both Winston Churchill, the Prime Minister of Great Britain, and Henry Morgenthau, the secretary of the U.S. Treasury, arguing that it would be better to just execute the Nazi leaders after a short hearing. They felt that the absence of a legal background for

Above: Britain's wartime leader, Winston Churchill (1874–1965), was unsure about the legality of holding trials for war crimes, but the Allies had previously declared that they intended to hold their enemies responsible for the war.

Among the senior Nazis in the dock at the Nuremberg trials were (front, from left): Hermann Göring, who was sentenced to death; Rudolph Hess, who was sentenced to prison; Joachim von Ribbentrop, who was sentenced to death; Karl Dönitz, who was sentenced to prison; and Baldur von Schirach, who was sentenced to prison.

Left: The Palace of Justice in Nuremberg was the site of the International Military Tribunal's trial of war criminals. The flags of the four prosecuting countries hang over the entrance.

these new war crimes would create difficulties. These objections were overruled, and an International Military Tribunal was created to conduct war crimes trials in Europe and Asia.

The Nuremberg Trials

The German city of Nuremberg was the site of the most important war trials after World War II. The ancient city had seen some of Hitler's most dramatic open-air rallies in the 1930s and had given rise to the Nuremberg Laws in 1935, which robbed Jews of their citizenship and forbade marriage with non-Jews. Although the city had been largely destroyed by Allied bombing, the Palace of Justice had remained standing, and this was where the trials took place.

Some commentators at the time were critical of the fact that people were being charged for offenses that were not criminal at the time they were committed. The charges were new ones. The British judge spoke of the "novel and experimental" nature of the proceedings, and all four judges—one each from the United States, France, Soviet Union, and Great Britain—agreed that the events that led to the trial were exceptional.

The American judge declared that "Civilization asks whether law is so laggard as to be utterly helpless to deal with crimes of this magnitude." The nature of the crime, genocide, was new from the legal point of view. No trial like this—accusing individuals as well as organizations (such as the SS, who were the elite troops of the Nazis, and the Gestapo, the Nazi state police) of crimes against humanity and crimes against peace—had been conducted before. Similar trials against Japanese war leaders opened in Tokyo, resulting in prison sentences and executions.

Although there is no doubt that Hermann Göring, onetime head of the Gestapo, was guilty of crimes against humanity, he made the observation in his prison cell that, "The victor will always be the judge and the vanquished the accused." At Nuremberg, the court did not allow any comparisons to be made with Allied actions, so it was not possible to discuss issues such as the treatment of Germany after World War I, or the Allied bombing of civilian targets in Germany toward the end of World War II. The judges and the prosecutors all came from the nations that had won the war, and they were only interested in war crimes committed by the defeated countries.

Hermann Göring awaits trial in his prison cell at Nuremberg

So It Has Come

"I am Major Neave, the officer appointed by the International Military Tribunal to serve upon you a copy of the indictment in which you are named as a defendant."

Göring's expression changed to a scowl, the look of a stage gangster, as the words were interpreted. I handed him a copy of the indictment which he took in silence. He listened as I said, "I am also asked to explain to you Article 16 of the Charter of the Tribunal."

A copy in German was handed to him.

"If you will look at paragraph (c). You have the right to conduct your own defense before the tribunal, or to have the assistance of counsel."

My words were correct and precise. Göring looked serious and depressed as I paused.

"So it has come," he said.

(From Airey Neave, *Nuremberg: A Personal Record*)

The trials at Nuremberg were conducted in four languages, lasted more than 10 months, and produced reams of documents, including films of death camps and artifacts from some of the camps. There were over 30 witnesses, and 43 volumes were required to publish the proceedings in 1946. More than 20 men were tried; they all pleaded not guilty. They were mostly chosen on the grounds that they represented the leadership of organizations responsible for the conduct of the war. There was no wish to prosecute individuals for particular war crimes, because this raised too many difficult legal and moral questions, including the rights and wrongs of following orders during a military conflict. In the end, 3 were acquitted, 12 were sentenced to hang, 3 received life imprisonment, and 4 were sentenced to between 10 and 20 years imprisonment.

Above: Airey Neave, who served at the Nuremberg trials, went on to become a politician in Great Britain.

After Nuremberg

The trials highlighted the fact that many doctors had committed war crimes by conducting forced experiments on prisoners in camps. This played a large part in the Declaration of Geneva in 1948, which was intended to update the Hippocratic Oath by obliging doctors to swear that "I will not permit considerations of religion, nationality, race…to intervene between my duty and my patients."

Some of those accused at Nuremberg claimed in their defense that they were only acting under the orders of Hitler and others. This argument was not accepted, and the principle was established that obeying orders cannot be used as an excuse for crimes against humanity. Many of the accused claimed that they simply did not know what was happening to the Jews. Walther Funk, the Nazi Minister of Economic Affairs, asked, "Do you think I had the slightest notion about gas wagons and such

Opposite top: The man on the left is Walther Funk (1890–1960), one of Hitler's chief advisers. He was sentenced to life imprisonment as a war criminal but released in 1957 because of ill health.

A Polish prosecution witness at Nuremberg, a former inmate of Ravensbruck, shows the deformed leg she suffered as a result of medical experiments in the camp.

horrors?" The court decided that he must have been aware of what was happening.

Eichmann's Arrest

Dramatic news came in 1960 that a high-ranking Nazi, one of the men chiefly responsible for the administration of the Holocaust, had been captured by Israeli secret agents and was awaiting trial in a Jerusalem jail. The prime minister of Israel stated that Adolf Eichmann was being put on trial to show the world that "there was an intention to exterminate a people… We are not out to punish Eichmann; there is no fit punishment."

Karl Adolf Eichmann

Eichmann was born in 1906 in Germany. While still young, his family moved to Austria. As a fanatical anti-Semite he became a member of the SS, the elite corps of the Nazi party. Eichmann organized anti-Jewish activities and took on the task of coordinating the deportation of Jews to the concentration camps and death camps.He was captured by American forces at the end of the war, but he kept his true identity hidden, and escaped from prison the same year. Five years later, he was living in Argentina, where Israeli agents tracked him down in 1960. He was seized by the Israelis and brought to Jerusalem to stand trial for "crimes against humanity." He was executed in 1962.

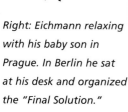

Right: Eichmann relaxing with his baby son in Prague. In Berlin he sat at his desk and organized the "Final Solution."

"Entirely Normal"

Eichmann played a major role in organizing the systematic mass murder of millions of men, women, and children across Europe. In 1941, he visited Auschwitz, the largest of the death camps, and discussed with the camp commandant the most efficient way of killing large numbers of people. They agreed on the use of gas chambers, which at that stage had not been installed at Auschwitz. Eichmann then worked out and coordinated the transportation program that brought trainloads of victims to the camps. It seems natural to think of such a person as mad, a psychopath driven by an insane hatred to commit murder on an unimaginable scale. This is what many people expected before they saw Eichmann, on television or in the flesh, as he stood in the Jerusalem courtroom.

Opposite: Simon Wiesenthal has tracked down Nazi war criminals for more than 50 years. As early as 1947, he successfully defeated an attempt by Eichmann's wife to have her husband declared officially dead.

Yet Eichmann did not look like a hate-filled psychopath. He did not look like a monster. The psychiatrist who examined him described him as "entirely normal...more normal than I feel myself after this examination." It continues to shock people that someone guilty of such awful crimes looked and behaved like an office worker. In a sense this is what he was, for he did not personally murder people. Eichmann said himself, "I sat at my desk and did my work."

Right: At his trial, Eichmann conducted his defense from within a bulletproof glass enclosure.

"A Demonic Superman"

Simon Wiesenthal described Eichmann as he appeared in court:

For nearly sixteen years I had thought of him practically every day and every night. In my mind I had built up the image of a demonic superman. Instead I saw a frail, nondescript, shabby fellow in a glass cell between two Israeli policemen; they looked more colorful and interesting than he did. Everything about Eichmann seemed drawn with charcoal: his grayish face, his balding head, his clothes. There was nothing demonic about him; he looked like a bookkeeper who is afraid to ask for a raise... Dressed in a cheap, dark suit, he seemed a cardboard figure, empty...

(Quoted in A. Levy, *The Wiesenthal File*)

Simon Wiesenthal

Simon Wiesenthal was born in 1908. During World War II, he survived imprisonment in a concentration camp, but 89 members of his family perished at the hands of the Nazis. After the war, he dedicated his life to gathering evidence against war criminals. He played a part in the capture of Eichmann, and the arrest of Franz Stangl, a death camp commandant who had fled to Brazil and who was brought to Germany to face trial in 1967. The Simon Wiesenthal Center was established in 1977, and its Museum of Tolerance in Los Angeles has become an international center for remembering the Holocaust.

Left: David Ben–Gurion, the Israeli prime minister at the time of Eichmann's trial, played a decisive role in having him brought back from South America to face charges as a war criminal.

Eichmann was found guilty of murder, though he was found not guilty of personally murdering anyone. He was responsible for murder because he sat behind a desk and organized the transportation and handled the paperwork that made the Holocaust possible. The Eichmann trial raised disturbing questions about how apparently normal people could be the perpetrators of genocide. Philosopher Hannah Arendt, whose reports of the trial shocked many Americans, famously said that he illustrated the sheer "banality" (commonplace nature) of evil.

Below: The trial of Eichmann made a new generation of young Israelis think about their past and about their relationship with the Jews of prewar Europe.

An Israeli Trial

The Holocaust did not receive a lot of attention in the early years of Israel's existence as a new state. By 1960, there was a noticeable division in Israeli society between native-born Israelis (called sabras) and those survivors from Europe who had settled there to start a new life. Many of the new generation of young Jews did not necessarily identify with European Jews, and many Holocaust survivors in Israel felt there was a lack of understanding of their plight. The trial of Eichmann changed this in a dramatic and permanent way.

The trial was very different from the Nuremberg trials because it took place in and was conducted by the state of Israel. It was suggested at the time that Eichmann should be prosecuted in an international court, and it was pointed out that not all of his victims were Jews. The Nazis had also set out to systematically exterminate Gypsies, and many thousands belonging to other minority groups, such as homosexuals, had also been murdered.

Even so, Israeli leaders were determined to keep the trial in their country, although sufficient evidence to convict Eichmann had already been collected during the Nuremberg trials. From a strictly legal point of view, it was not necessary to have 56 survivors of the Holocaust come to the courtroom in Jerusalem to relate details of their experiences in Nazi-occupied Europe. But Israeli leaders wanted the details of the Holocaust to be made public because they wanted their citizens to have an awareness of the Holocaust. The Israeli prime minister David Ben–Gurion, explained that young Israelis "had only a faint echo of the atrocious crime, and the facts must be made known to them."

Below: One of the witnesses at Eichmann's trial, Leana Neumann, pointed to bullet holes in her arm in the course of providing first-hand evidence of the Holocaust.

Many prosecution witnesses were Holocaust survivors who came to the courtroom to record their painful memories of what had happened to them and their families. There were many dramatic scenes, such as when a witness described a visit to the death camp at Treblinka—the ground had been covered with bones and skulls and countless thousands of children's shoes.

A Pair of Shoes

A person in the Jerusalem courtroom described what happened when a witness held up the tiny pair of shoes he had brought back from Treblinka:

For seemingly endless seconds, we were gripped by the spell cast by this symbol of all that was left of a million children. Time stood still, while each in his own way tried to fit flesh to the shoes, multiply by a million, and spin the reel back from death, terror and tears to the music and gay laughter and the animated joy of youngsters in European cities and villages before the Nazis marched in.

(Quoted in Tim Cole, *Images of the Holocaust*)

The Eichmann trial influenced the way a new generation of Israelis began to see themselves and their identity as Jews. Being a citizen of Israel now also meant being a member of a nation that had undergone a wholesale slaughter of its people. The victims of the Holocaust were identified with Israel. This became clear when the chief prosecutor, a member of the Israeli government, declared in his opening speech that he was speaking on behalf of the six million victims of Nazism.

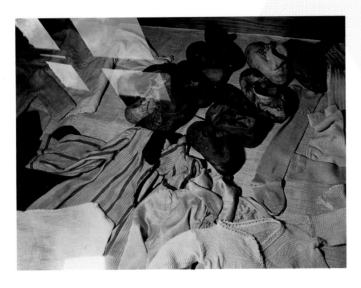

Left: Children's shoes and other personal belongings left behind at Auschwitz by some of the camp's nameless victims give stark testimony to the horrors of the Holocaust.

I Will Be Their Spokesperson

Gideon Hausner, Chief Prosecutor:

When I stand before you here, Judges of Israel, to lead the Prosecution of Adolf Eichmann, I am not standing alone. With me are six million accusers. But they cannot rise to their feet and point an accusing finger towards him who sits in the dock and cry:

"I accuse." For their ashes are piled up on the hills of Auschwitz and the fields of Treblinka, and are strewn in the forests of Poland. Their blood cries out, but their voice is not heard. Therefore I will be their spokesman and in their name I will unfold the awesome indictment.

(Quoted in M. Pearlman, *The Capture and Trial of Adolf Eichmann*)

Left: Gideon Hausner, chief prosecutor at the Eichmann trial said: "It is not an individual that is in the dock at his historic trial, and not the Nazi regime alone, but anti-Semitism throughout history."

The trial was important for Israeli self-identity because Israel was still a very young nation. Israeli political leaders were keen to use the trial to bring home to their citizens the horror and the magnitude of the Holocaust. There is some justice in the fact that Eichmann, a person murderously prejudiced against Jews, ended up helping to reinforce a sense of identity for Israeli Jews and their new homeland.

From the Cold War to the Present

Eichmann was just one of many former Nazis who managed to evade justice in the years after the defeat of Germany. There were an estimated 100,000 people in Europe who could have faced charges at Nuremberg, but only about one in ten was ever prosecuted. Trials that took place later were known as Subsequent Nuremberg Proceedings, but by 1949 they had ended. The reason was that almost as soon as World War II was over, the Cold War began. The Cold War, resulting from conflict between the United States and the Soviet Union, led to the division of Germany in 1949 (into the East German Democratic Republic and the West German Federal Republic). There was now growing distrust between two superpowers that had only recently fought together as allies.

The United States wanted to strengthen western Europe against what it saw as a threat from Soviet communism. Bearing this in mind, it did not seem advisable to prosecute large numbers of Germans, especially those in positions of influence and power. Such people could play a useful role in creating social, economic, and political stability in West Germany, and many were protected from prosecution for this reason.

Now that the Cold War is over, some of the issues that were buried in the late 1940s and 1950s have come to the surface. But, as with the decision not to prosecute many of German war criminals after the war, the moral claim for justice still has to compete with political self-interest on the part of other governments and organizations. This conflict between morality and politics can also be seen in the resistance that many Holocaust survivors encounter when they make claims for compensation for their suffering.

Below: In September 1961, parents from West Berlin hold up their twins to show them to their grandparents on the other side of the newly built Berlin Wall. The wall came to symbolize the Cold War between the United States and the Soviet Union.

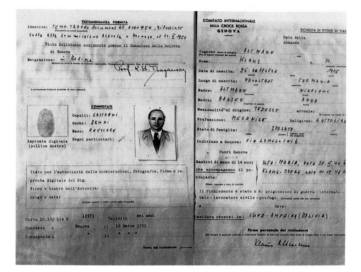

Left: After the war, U.S. intelligence services recruited Klaus Barbie, former head of the Gestapo in the French city of Lyon. In return for his services as a spy, they arranged for him to leave Germany in 1951 and move to Bolivia. On these travel documents his name is given as Klaus Altmann.

Compensation Claims Against Germany

Since 1945, Germany has paid out more than $45 billion in compensation to Nazi victims. Holocaust survivors can qualify for German monthly pensions of around $250, but the issue has still not been fully settled. Although Eastern Europe was the main site of the Holocaust, the Cold War prevented most of the survivors there from benefiting from compensation paid by what was then West Germany. Even though the Cold War is now over, the majority of Holocaust survivors in the east have received very little or no compensation at all. Those campaigning for compensation for the estimated 15,000 Holocaust survivors in eastern Europe point out that Germany is paying pensions to as many as 50,000 Germans and non-Germans who are suspected of involvement in war crimes. Many of those receiving pensions are former members of military units described as criminal at Nuremberg. Critics also point out that more than 800 Germans living in Argentina, Brazil and Chile—popular havens for Nazis fleeing after the war —are receiving pensions.

Above: Klaus Barbie was finally tried in France in 1987. Found guilty of responsibility for the deaths of 4,000 people and the deportation of 7,500 more, he was sentenced to life imprisonment.

At the end of 1999, Germany agreed to compensate family members of those who were forced by the Nazis to work in German factories. Millions of Jews and non-Germans were compelled to work, unpaid, in factories for private companies. The agreement makes a distinction between "slave labor" (defined as those from concentration camps) and "forced laborers" (who lived in labor camps). Under the agreement, survivors or family members receive a sum of $3,000–$8,000, in exchange for a guarantee not to file future claims against German companies, such as Volkswagen and Daimler-Chrysler, that profited from such labor.

Other Claims

Claims for compensation have also been filed against Swiss banks accused of laundering money that was stolen from Jews by the Nazis and deposited in Switzerland. As much as $7 billion may be lying, unclaimed, in Swiss bank vaults. Although Switzerland remained neutral during World War II, the country served as the Nazis' banker, and some Swiss financial institutions had close business links with Nazi Germany.

Below left: This German factory was one of many that used forced labor during the war.

Below right: Volkswagen's German corporate headquarters are in the city of Wolfsburg. Volkswagen was just one of the many large German companies that used forced labor during the Nazi regime.

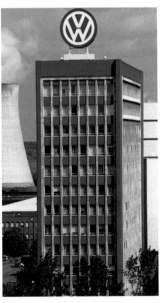

A Modern Hero

Christopher Meili was a business school student who worked in a Swiss bank as a nightwatchman in order to help support his family. One night in January 1997, while patrolling the underground chambers of the bank, he came across some old ledgers in a shredding room. Meili recognized the name of a bank that had flourished during the war and decided to smuggle out some of the papers that were due to be shredded. He had followed stories in the news about Swiss banks and the Nazis, and he knew that a law had been passed forbidding banks to destroy material relating to the war.

The 59 yellowing pages that he stuffed under his uniform contained dates and names that forced the bank to admit it was holding money that rightfully belonged to Jews: "I thought only very briefly about what I was seeing—I could only spend 20 minutes in the room before activating the alarms—and decided to take some of the documents away with me." When the documents were made public, Meili, who is not Jewish, received hate mail and death threats.

(From the *Manchester Guardian*, May 14, 1997)

Right: Christopher Meili gives evidence to the U.S. Senate Banking Committee in Washington, D.C.

Jewish families had also deposited money in Swiss banks before the war, and at first Switzerland refused to consider paying any compensation to them. This led to a U.S. government report being written on relations between Swiss banks and Nazi Germany and what happened to Jewish assets after the war. The report concluded that Switzerland, and other neutral countries, such as Sweden, Portugal, and Turkey, benefited by working with Nazi Germany. The report also criticized the U.S. government for doing very little to try and have the looted assets returned to their owners. As was the case with German war criminals, the unfolding Cold War with the Soviet Union was seen as more important than moral questions about stolen gold. The Swiss case has led to banks in other countries releasing funds deposited by Jews who fled the Holocaust. Barclays Bank has recently agreed to pay money to survivors who can prove that their accounts in France were seized after the German invasion.

In 1999, the first claim for compensation was made against the Polish government for taking property belonging to Jews. Peter Koppenheim, who is 68 and lives in Manchester, England, is using the courtroom in the hope that, if he is successful, his case will allow hundreds of others in similar situations to do the same. He claims that the Polish government transferred large amounts of Jewish property to non-Jewish citizens. His family was allowed to leave Poland in 1939, after paying a hefty Jewish exit tax (a special tax imposed on Jews wishing to leave the

Above: Gold bars line a Swiss bank vault. The issue of Jewish assets held by Swiss banks has forced the Swiss to confront their country's role during the war.

Left: Peter Koppenheim, whose grandfather did not leave Breslau in Poland because he refused to accept that Jews would be deliberately killed. He died in the ghetto along with thousands of others. Koppenheim's claim for compensation is expected to generate hundreds of similar cases.

International Courts

The Nuremberg trials established the important principle that people could be held legally accountable for their conduct during a war. In recent years this principle has been extended. As a result of the war in the former Yugoslavia between 1991 and 1995, an international war crimes tribunal was established to investigate and bring to justice those held responsible for crimes of genocide. The International Court of Justice, administered by the United Nations, deals with cases of conflict between states, and the European Court of Human Rights deals with international law as it affects European countries. There are calls for a new international court to be established so that crimes of genocide anywhere in the world can be investigated.

country), but they had to abandon their real-estate business. Koppenheim plans to donate any money received to charity, but he wants to establish the principle of compensation for past wrongs because, he says, "There are many other people who suffered a similar fate to me and my family."

Left: The Peace Palace in the Hague in the Netherlands is the home of the International Court of Justice

CONTROVERSIES

THE SEEKING of compensation has less to do with money than with the need to bring to justice those who carry some responsibility for what happened. However, German companies and Swiss banks have only acted in response to the threat of court action. Courts of law have thus become the battleground for claims of justice arising from acts of genocide and other serious abuses of human rights.

The case of Konrad Kalejs, a Latvian who was allowed to leave Great Britain in 2000 despite being suspected of Nazi war crimes, caused controversy because the case was not taken to the courts. As time passes, gathering and presenting evidence is becoming more difficult. This was the reason given for not prosecuting Kalejs. More than 50 years have passed since the end of the Holocaust, and people who played a part, whether victims, witnesses, or perpetrators, are now elderly and sometimes ill. Is

Below: Before Konrad Kalejs arrived in Great Britain, he had tried to settle in Canada. He is shown here, with an unidentified companion, trying to avoid being photographed outside a courtroom in Toronto, Canada, in 1997.

it time to give up the pursuit of those who helped carry out the Holocaust? Or should those responsible always be prosecuted because no one should be allowed to escape justice for such a terrible crime?

Konrad Kalejs

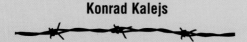

Konrad Kalejs was discovered living in Great Britain in 2000. He had previously been deported from the United States and Canada for involvement in wartime atrocities. Kalejs is a Latvian who was second in command of a unit that worked with the Nazis in murdering 30,000 people, mostly Jews. The holder of an Australian passport, Kalejs was allowed to leave Great Britain despite protests calling for him to be deported to Latvia to stand trial. Anti-Semitic Latvians helped the Nazis extensively in the extermination of the Jews but the country has not prosecuted a single Nazi criminal since becoming independent.

Did the Allies Ignore the Holocaust?

A 20-page document released in 1999 shows that the Allies were officially made aware of the Holocaust as early as December 1942, much earlier than previously thought. Franklin D. Roosevelt, president of the United States, met Jewish leaders at the end of 1942, and chilling details of the situation in Nazi Europe were disclosed. The report was passed on to the British government, which had received similar information months earlier, but nothing was ever done by either Great Britain or the United States. The most charitable explanation for the lack of action by the United States is that the country was preoccupied by pressing military matters and that winning the war was seen to be the priority. It is also possible that the plight of Jews simply did not strike some high-ranking officials as a matter for urgent concern. Similarly, various reasons have been put forward to explain why the Allies never bombed Auschwitz, something that became very possible in 1944 after the capture of Italian airfields. Their lack of action remains controversial.

Below: Jan Karski was a Polish member of the underground who made secret visits to the Warsaw ghetto and reported on the situation of Polish Jews to both Churchill and Roosevelt in 1942.

A Meeting at the White House, 1942

MEMORANDUM SUBMITTED TO THE PRESIDENT
OF THE UNITED STATES
At the White House
On Tuesday, December 8, 1942 At Noon
By a Delegation of representatives of Jewish Organizations

Almost two million Jews of Nazi Europe have been exterminated through mass murder, planned starvation, deportation, slave labor and epidemic in disease-ridden ghettos, penal labor colonies and slave reservations created for their destruction by the German Government and its satellites…

The slaughter of trainloads of Jewish adults and children in great crematoriums at Oswiecim [Auschwitz] near Cracow is confirmed by eye-witnesses in reports which recently reached Jerusalem…

Left: According to a recently released document, President Franklin D. Roosevelt (1882–1945) was made aware of the death camps as early as December 1942.

It has been said that Great Britain could not allow its knowledge to be made public because it would have put at risk the intelligence-gathering agency that was successfully decoding German communications. British officials may also have been affected by their own anti-Semitism, which may have made them

Left: Bletchley Park in the British countryside was a center for deciphering German coded messages that provided a source of information about the unfolding Holocaust.

unwilling to accept the truth of what they were being told. There could also have been a reluctance to publicize stories that would have encouraged Jewish emigration to Palestine. At the time, Great Britain was restricting such emigration.

The failure of the Allies to act has been defended on the grounds that the only way to bring the Holocaust to an end was by the military defeat of Germany. By making this their priority, the Allies were working toward the end of the concentration and death camps. One scholar, John Fox, has argued that "a global war had to be fought and won, and hard as it may sound, the fate of civilians sited in places way beyond the reach of any Allied forces really had to be placed on a low priority." This may be true, but it does not rule out the possibility, or the likelihood, that the Allies were also slow to react to the Holocaust because they were not particularly bothered by the fate of European Jews.

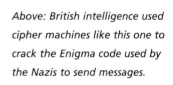

Above: British intelligence used cipher machines like this one to crack the Enigma code used by the Nazis to send messages.

Left: Nazi intelligence officers send communications using the Enigma code. Would publicity about the death camps have given away the fact that the British had broken the Enigma code?

The Role of the Roman Catholic Church

THE ROMAN Catholic Church's response to the Holocaust is also the subject of controversy. Despite the fact that Pope Pius XII was very well-informed about events in Europe, he never publicly condemned the Nazis. He did not even speak out against the rounding up of 8,000 Jews in Rome in 1943. The previous pope had attacked Nazism in 1937, but Pius XII halted the publication of his predecessor's statement condemning Hitler's policies, and he has been accused of indifference to the plight of the Jews. The Church approved of the Nazis' anti-communism and did not appear to acknowledge its moral duty to stand up against the persecution and murder of Jews. In fact, in the predominantly Roman Catholic states of Slovakia and Croatia, a number of bishops supported government policies of genocide.

Below: A strong appeal by Pius XII might have silenced those Catholic bishops who chose to actively support the Nazis. Yet despite countless appeals, the Pope remained silent.

Seeking the Truth

The Vatican (the papal government in Vatican City) has recently announced that it will open some of its wartime records to a team of Catholic and Jewish historians. The Vatican has defended Pope Pius XII by saying he did not dare to speak out for fear of further endangering the lives of Jews and Catholics in Europe. Critics point out that the Vatican could hardly have made life any more dangerous for Jews, and that to remain silent on such a subject went against everything the Church stood for. Some historians say that opening up just some of the Vatican's records will not settle the controversy.

There were heroic examples of self-sacrifice on the part of a few individual priests and members of Protestant churches in Germany who tried to save Jews. Nevertheless, the general record of the Christian churches' response to the Holocaust is depressing. Many people feel that the Lutheran Church of Germany and the Vatican could and should have done more and that they failed in their duty. The controversy about this continues.

In March 2000, Pope John Paul II made a historic trip to Israel and visited the Yad Vashem Holocaust memorial and the Western Wall in Jerusalem. Just before this visit, the Pope made a plea for forgiveness of the Catholic Church's past sins, including its treatment of Jews, and said: "We are deeply saddened by the behavior of those who in the course of history have caused these children of yours [the Jews] to suffer." There was, however, no actual reference to Pope Pius XII or to the Holocaust. This led to criticism from some Jewish leaders in Israel and the United States who had hoped for a more specific apology.

Above: Pope John Paul II leaves a prayer at the Western Wall, a place of pilgrimage sacred to the Jewish people, in Jerusalem in 2000.

Willing Executioners?

A best-selling book, *Hitler's Willing Executioners: Ordinary Germans and the Holocaust*, has caused controversy since it was published in 1996. The author, historian Daniel Goldhagen, claims that many ordinary Germans were so anti-Semitic that they willingly aided Hitler's plans for the Holocaust. Citing in particular the actions of the *Einsatzgruppen*, Goldhagen attempts to demonstrate that many Germans were willing to carry out violent and sadistic acts against Jews even without compulsion from higher authorities.

This book has been severely criticized by other historians who claim that the evidence shows a more complicated picture of German society. Most Germans were not Jew-hating fanatics, they argue. It was Hitler's monopoly of power, and the course of the war, that allowed the Nazis to perpetrate the Holocaust.

The controversy has a wider significance because of the way in which the Holocaust is now studied. The idea that the Nazis were perverted individuals in the grip of an insane anti-Semitism does not help us understand how and why the Holocaust happened, why other genocides have happened before and since, and why they may happen again.

Above: Daniel Goldhagen is the author of Hitler's Willing Executioners

Below: Yasser Arafat, the Palestinian leader, addresses his people

Denying History

In 2000, the author David Irving sued the publisher and author of a book that accused him of denying the history of the Holocaust. By bringing the case to court, Irving had a public platform to argue that there had never been any systematic destruction of European Jews by Hitler's Germany. Although Irving admitted that places like Auschwitz had existed, he claimed they were just brutal labor camps where atrocities were sometimes committed. Irving rejects the evidence of the thousands of witnesses and claims that incriminating documents are forgeries.

Irving lost his case and the judge condemned him as "an anti-Semitic, racist, active pro-Nazi who distorts history." One newspaper commented after the trial that the case was a "victory for memory," emphasizing the fact that the Holocaust took place within living memory and that witnesses are still alive.

Seeing the Holocaust only in terms of the Jews as victims can also be used to protect Israel from criticism over its treatment of the Arabs. Israel's justifiable claim that it must protect its Jewish citizens does not override the rights of Arabs. [The Holocaust can protect Israel because those who criticize the country can be accused of anti-Semitism. This becomes a way of avoiding questions about the rights of Palestinians.] The Holocaust ought to make Israel especially aware of the rights of dispossessed people but the Palestinians feel the opposite is true. The whole question of how to remember the Holocaust has become deeply controversial and entangled with other issues.

Above: David Irving is perhaps the most well-known of the so-called Holocaust deniers. One of the lawyers at Irving's trial commented, "Mr. Irving calls himself a historian. The truth is, however, that he is not a historian at all. To put it bluntly, he is a liar."

REMEMBERING THE HOLOCAUST

F OR MORE than 15 years after the end of the World War II, survivors tended to remain silent about their experiences; what had happened was often too painful to recall. And, even if they had wanted to talk, there was little encouragement to do so. One British prisoner of war, who had ended up in Auschwitz, was interviewed for a BBC television history program. He remembered returning to Great Britain and giving a talk about the gas chambers. His audience showed no interest, partly not believing the truth of what he said and partly not wishing to believe it. There was a considerable amount of guilt, in the United States as well as Europe, about not having done much to help the Jews.

The End of Silence

The Eichmann trial in the early 1960s increased public awareness of the Holocaust, especially for Israeli Jews but also for the wider world. A movie company from the United States filmed the entire trial and edited highlights were shown on American television. Soon after the trial the term Holocaust began to be used regularly and recognized by the public.

Above: This memorial window was created by Moshe Galili, a Holocaust survivor. The Hebrew script at the top means "The People of Israel Shall Live."

Right: A former inmate returns to Treblinka death camp in Claude Lanzmann's documentary film Shoah.

In the late 1970s, a television mini-series, *Holocaust*, attempted to depict the experience of Europe's Jews by focusing on a fictional Jewish family. Lasting nearly 10 hours, over four evening broadcasts, the series was watched by more than 120 million Americans. The following year, when it was shown in West Germany, 14 million people watched it. The series, especially in Germany, made the Holocaust a topic of conversation among people who previously had little knowledge of the subject.

Nowadays there are memorials to the Holocaust in most large cities across the United States, and every year around 6 million people visit the major Holocaust museums around the world. The Holocaust is remembered in books (by authors such as Primo Levi and Elie Wiesel), works of art, documentary films, Hollywood movies, museums, and monuments.

These many different memorials represent society's attempts to find meaning in the murder of 6 million Jews. Different meanings have been suggested, and concern has been expressed over some of the ways in which the Holocaust has been remembered.

Below: The film Life Is Beautiful *raised the question of whether comedy should ever find its way into a film about the Holocaust.*

Film and Reality

A 1998 Italian film, *Life Is Beautiful*, a fictional account of a father and his child in a Nazi camp, was criticized for not fully confronting the horror of what happened in the camps. *Shoah*, on the other hand, distilled 350 hours of interviews into one long film that focused purely on people who experienced the Holocaust, from train engineers and guards to one of the two Jews who survived the murder of 400,000 at Chelmno death camp. In 1974, *The Odessa File* told the story of Nazis who sought to smuggle stolen Jewish gold out of Germany after 1945 and worked to establish a new Nazi movement. It was not until 1996 that documents uncovered in the United States proved that such a group had really existed.

Hollywood's Holocaust

Made in 1993, the film *Schindler's List* tells the true story of Oskar Schindler, a German businessman who saved the lives of more than 1,000 Jews by employing them in Czechoslovakia as workers in his ceramics factory. Those whose names were on the list—who were permitted to leave Poland with Schindler—would otherwise have perished in the death camps. Directed by Steven Spielberg, the film was based on a historical novel, also called *Schindler's List*, by the Australian writer Thomas Keneally.

The hero of the film and the novel, Oskar Schindler, was not a particularly admirable character before being caught up in the events of World War II. By his own admission, he was not especially

Opposite: This still is from Schindler's List, a film watched by 25 million Americans in movie theaters and 65 million when it was shown on television.

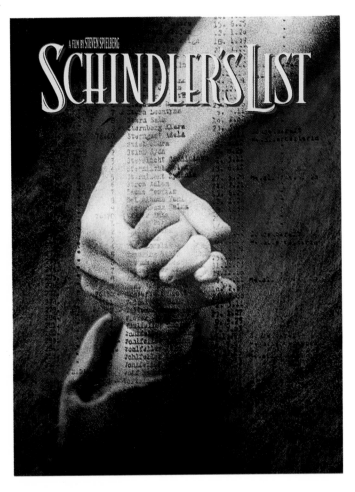

Left: The poster for Schindler's List. In many ways it was a classic Hollywood film about an action hero who "saves the world."

concerned with the policies of Germany's Nazi regime. A womanizer and a carouser, he was concerned most of all with making his business a success. At first, he *was* interested most in employing Jews in his factory because they were a source of cheap labor.

In time, however, as Schindler became aware of what was happening to the Jews in Poland and elsewhere in Russia, his conscience began to bother him. He took it upon himself to employ as many Jews as possible, even more than he needed in the factory, knowing that those on his list of employees would be safe from transportation to the death camps.

Below: The Australian author Thomas Keneally told the story of Oskar Schindler in a 1982 novel, but it was the film version that brought it to world attention.

Schindler's character is contrasted with that of Amon Goeth, the real-life commandant at the Plaznow concentration camp in Poland. While Schindler does what he can to save as many Jews as possible, even while knowing that by doing so he cannot stop the Holocaust, Goeth is portrayed as a sadist who enjoys shooting at the prisoners in the camp just for fun.

Despite its undeniable power, *Schindler's List* has been criticized for being a "feel-good" movie about the Holocaust. Such critics argue that by focusing on a heroic figure and 1,100 "saved" Jews, rather than on the 6 million Jews who were killed, the film somehow softens the tragedy of the Holocaust. Supporters of the film argue that it shows that even when faced by overwhelming evil, individuals may still act in a way that is moral and even heroic.

Cookbooks and Superman

As the events of the Holocaust are commemorated more and more, there is a danger that this terrible episode in history will begin to lose some of its impact. If such a serious subject becomes too commercialized it can also become trivialized. In 1996, when a Holocaust cookbook appeared on sale in New York, this was seen by some as an indication of how the tragedy of a genocide had become something marketable.

Schindler's List is mostly shot in black and white but there is a dramatic use of color when a girl in a red dress appears. In the Polish town of Cracow, tourists now visit the street where Steven Spielberg filmed this girl in a red dress. In 1998, the comic-book hero Superman traveled back in time to Nazi-occupied Poland, proclaiming "I'm not one to interfere with the governments of the world, but I can't turn a blind eye and let these fascist bullies exterminate everyone they don't like."

Below: Children in Rwanda watch a wounded Tutsi woman, just one victim of genocidal attacks by Hutu militias.

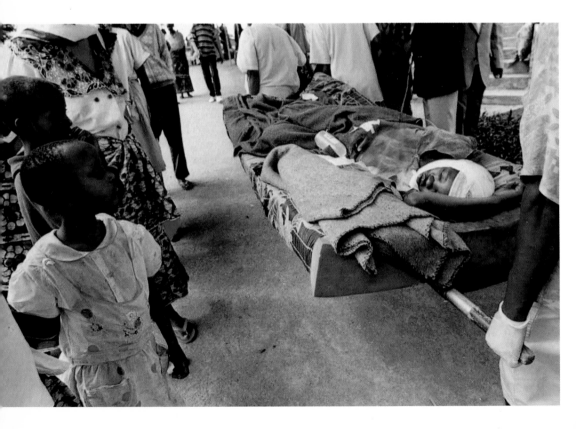

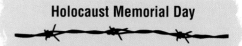

Holocaust Memorial Day

The anniversary of the liberation of Auschwitz, January 27, has been declared Holocaust Memorial Day in Great Britain. Not everyone thinks that such a day is necessarily a good idea. One director of a Holocaust Memorial Centre in Great Britain wondered whether "children will get to sing songs about the Holocaust and reduce 20th century mass death to the status of National No Smoking Day." There is also the argument that, unique as the Holocaust was, it would be better to remember all those who have been victims of genocide throughout the world.

Does the Superman story help to increase young people's awareness of the Holocaust, or is it an example of the trivialization of what happened? The same question could be asked about a "Holocaust Quiz" on Israeli television where young contestants gained points for correctly answering questions about the death camps.

Above left: Steven Spielberg, director of Schindler's List, *has gone on to support the Shoah Foundation and its various Holocaust-related projects.*

Genocide Day

Hundreds of thousands of people became victims of Stalin's genocide against ethnic groups toward the end of World War II, and there have since been many massacres of racial minorities—in the former Yugoslavia, East Timor, Rwanda, and other countries. In view of this, some people have suggested that January 27 in Britain should mark a memorial day for the victims of all genocide. As Laurence Rees, writer and television producer, has said:

How do you explain to a Kalmyk family whose beloved child died in the freezing conditions of a Siberian exile that their loss is somehow not worth remembering as much as the Jewish child who died on the same day in a Nazi death camp? Both were killed unjustly. Both were victims of genocide in the same war…The answer must be to make Holocaust Day Genocide Day.

(Quoted in the British newspaper the *Independent*, October 26, 1999)

Preserving Memories

About 5,000 people visit the Holocaust Memorial Museum in Washington, D.C., every day. Some 2,000 people enter the gates of the main Auschwitz camp in eastern Poland, and about the same number line up daily to visit the house in Amsterdam where the Jewish teenager, Anne Frank, hid and wrote her famous diary. Different countries remember the Holocaust in different ways. The museum in Washington, D.C., contrasts the horrors of the death camps with the liberal values of modern America, and the first exhibits inside the museum remind visitors of the American liberation of some of the camps. Yad Vashem, the major Holocaust museum in Israel, focuses more on the heroic resistance of Jews and Israel's legacy.

In Poland, Auschwitz has become a major tourist attraction, and some of its real history has been obscured. A gas chamber and crematorium have been poorly reconstructed, using parts of the originals, and they have not been placed on the site of the main extermination camp. The actual main death camp was situated some distance away from the camp where today's visitors congregate. Some people have used the way Auschwitz is preserved to claim, untruthfully, that what took place there has been exaggerated.

Above: The Labyrinth of Names is part of the Yad Vashem Holocaust Museum in Israel

Below: The entrance to Auschwitz. Are the 700,000 people who visit every year pilgrims or tourists—or both?

"Look at the faces"

Elie Wiesel, a writer who survived Auschwitz, recorded the way he would like to have the past remembered:

...a kind of hall and we enter that hall to be covered with photos...of Treblinka...From all the far corners of exile and memory people have come there, to die there...And then I would like maybe a voice or a guide to speak softly, to whisper..."look at the faces, look at them well." This is the way I would begin... I want those people who go there to come out 2,000 years old.

(Quoted in E.T. Linenthal, *Preserving Memory: The Struggle to Create America's Holocaust Museum*)

Remembering the Holocaust, and drawing meaning from it, is very important, but it is not as easy as it sounds. The fact that people buy badges with the slogan "Never Again" at Holocaust museums such as the one in Washington, does not mean that it could not or will not happen again. There is a danger of the Holocaust starting to lose its meaning through too much commercialism and too many museums.

Below: The ruins of crematorium no. 2, at the site of the main death camp at Auschwitz, is some distance away from the complex that people visit today.

NEVER AGAIN?

THERE IS, sadly, nothing new about people being persecuted to death. The murder of the Jews is not what makes the Holocaust unique. Half a million Gypsies were also systematically murdered. As a proportion of their total population, this was equal to the Jewish genocide. At least 250,000 mentally or physically disabled people were also victims of genocide. Over three million Soviet prisoners of war were killed because their nationality condemned them as *Untermenschen* (subhumans), and around two million Gentile Poles died for the same reason. Thousands of political opponents of Nazism—mainly communists, socialists, and trade unionists—were also killed. In terms of individual suffering, all these victims and those of other genocides are alike.

Below: This Gypsy couple, photographed in an open area in the Belzec death camp, later died in the gas chamber. Prejudice against Gypsies and Jews continues in Europe to this day.

United Nations Genocide Convention 1948

ARTICLE 11

Genocide means any of the following acts committed with intent to destroy, in whole or in part, a national, ethnic, racial or religious group, such as:

a) killing members of the group;

b) causing serious bodily or mental harm to members of the group;

c) deliberately inflicting on the group conditions of life calculated to bring about its physical destruction in whole or part;

d) imposing measures intended to prevent births within the group;

e) forcibly transferring children of the group to another group…

Persecution Under Stalin

While the Holocaust was in progress, massive persecution was also taking place under Joseph Stalin in the Soviet Union. Entire ethnic communities were uprooted from their homes and transported, in cattle trucks to Siberia and other remote corners of the Soviet Union. More than a million people were transported and one in four died from the cold and lack of food on the journey alone.

Stalin wanted revenge on ethnic groups that had cooperated with the invading Nazis, and he chose to punish everyone within that group, guilty or innocent. He also used relocation to eliminate possible sources of national discontent within The Soviet Union, which was home to dozens of ethnic and religious minorities.In this way, the Chechens, Kalmyks, Tatars, Balkars, Karachai, and many others all became victims. Even loyal members of these ethnic groups serving in the Soviet army were not spared. Stalin did not care how many died on the journey to Siberia, and state power was used to move them against their will, but physically exterminating every one of them was not the main intention.

The Uniqueness of the Holocaust

Part of what makes the Holocaust unique is that one group of people, the Jews, were singled out for total extermination, and that this was the specific policy of a modern state. The Holocaust was also different from other genocides because it was a systematic extermination that employed civil servants, lawyers, doctors, engineers and a host of other professions. Jews were denounced as an inferior people without rights, and the genocide proceeded with the assistance of many and the indifference of most others.

Above: The Russian novelist Alexsandr Solzhenitsyn, who criticized Stalin's government in his books, was one of millions who had been sent to forced labor camps in the Soviet Union.

The Holocaust was a unique event in many ways, but the act of genocide is not itself unique. Hitler is reported to have justified the cold-blooded killing of Poles by exclaiming, "Who, after all, talks nowadays of the extermination of the Armenians?" Around 1.5 million Armenians had been systematically killed by Turkey during World War I. There are also a number of disturbing similarities between aspects of the Holocaust and other events that have taken place since then.

"Man's Inhumanity to Man"

The Nazis began their persecution of Jews by introducing a series of laws that restricted their rights, denied their citizenship, and encouraged racist attitudes. The apartheid system that operated in South Africa between 1948 and 1994 also used racist laws to exclude black people from the full rights of citizenship. Jews were forbidden to enter Germany's parks or public swimming pools, while in South Africa under apartheid, blacks faced severe restrictions on virtually all aspects of behavior. This did not lead to genocide in South Africa, but the German and South African regimes shared some characteristics.

Below: After the Holocaust, racism was openly practiced in white-governed South Africa.

During the 1970s Cambodia was the site of genocide. Approximately two million Cambodians were killed by the ruling party, which was known as the Khmer Rouge.

Left: Kampuchea, as Cambodia was then called, was so isolated from the rest of the world in the 1970s that it took some time for the scale of the genocide there to be realized.

Left: In 1982, many hundreds of Arabs were massacred at the Palestinian Shattila refugee camp in south Lebanon. The occupying Israeli armed forces dropped flares at night to help the Lebanese Christian militiamen who carried out the killings.

American bombing of the country during the Vietnam War had disrupted Cambodian society, allowing the Khmer Rouge to emerge as the most powerful force in the nation. The Khmer Rouge ruthlessly persecuted its own people, creating labor camps where about one-quarter of the country's population died from disease, starvation, or execution. Again, there are similarities with the way Jews found themselves isolated within their own countries and powerless to resist what seemed too horrible to be real.

In Bosnia, Serbia, and other parts of former Yugoslavia genocidal acts have been conducted as part of what has been termed "ethnic cleansing." The term "ethnic cleansing" is often used as a euphemism (a polite expression) for genocide. The process is the same: identifying a whole group of people as undesirable because of their race or ethnicity, and targeting them for destruction.

Because Israel was established as a specifically Jewish state, its creation, and the wars that followed, resulted in Israeli occupation of much territory claimed by Arabs and the ultimate displacement of millions of Palestinian refuges. Some Arabs argue that Israel has treated the Palestinians similarly to the way Nazis treated the Jews.

Below: Palestinian women, at the Jabalya refugee camp in the Israeli-occupied West Bank, protest plans to build houses for Israeli settlers on their land.

Racism

Racism (a belief in the superiority of a particular race) was a powerful and constant factor in the unfolding tragedy of the Holocaust. Many Germans saw themselves as being at the top of the racial order, with Slavic people such as the Poles and Russians below them and the Jews at the very bottom. In scientific terms, of course, race is a meaningless concept. There are no inherent biological differences between the so-called races. What people call "race" are really just differences in appearance (especially skin color), language, and cultural beliefs, including religion. Strictly speaking, being a Jew is a matter of religious belief or cultural identification. What Hitler and the Nazis succeeded in doing was to convert religious anti-Semitism to racial anti-Semitism. Today in many countries, there are mainstream political parties that advocate racist policies. Such parties are said to belong to the far or extreme right.

Left: In 2000, the leader of Austria's extreme right Freedom Party, Jörg Haider, became a member of the coalition government.

Less Than One Percent

Less than 1 percent of the total population of non-Jews under Nazi occupation helped to rescue Jews. This tiny percentage represents not just German people but also the ordinary citizens of France, Poland, and other occupied countries who did little to prevent what was happening to the Jews. It may be that very often people did not fully realize what was happening, but from 1942 onward many must have suspected the truth.

Eichmann's excuse at his trial was that he was just doing his job, but such an attitude can lead to an unthinking obedience to authority. An English writer, C.P. Snow, made the observation that "when you look at the long and gloomy history of man you will find more hideous crimes have been committed in the name of obedience than have ever been committed in the name of rebellion." The Holocaust bears this out.

Lessons of the Holocaust

The uncomfortable idea that genocide is carried out not just by psychopaths but by so-called "ordinary people" is one of the many lessons to emerge from the Holocaust. It is no longer possible to think that "it couldn't happen here." The Holocaust has seriously weakened the idea that modern societies have progressed to the point where such actions are unthinkable.

Below: Jean-Marie Le Pen, leader of France's extreme right-wing National Front Party, won 15 percent of the national vote in a recent presidential election.

Somewhere Along the Line

For some people, it is more comfortable to believe that Eichmann and people like him must have been insane. That way it becomes easy to believe that we share no similarities with such people. To recognize similarities between people like Eichmann and the majority of ordinary citizens is disturbing. Moshe Pearlman, an Israeli citizen, watching Eichmann at his trial in Israel, came to this realization:

And one was suddenly struck by the fearsome thought that the men who bullied and raped and tortured and shot and burned and gassed millions of innocent people were ordinary folk—just like any of us—who had gone wrong somewhere along the line and had been led into a strange world, a world without principle, without scruple and without compassion.

(M. Pearlman, *The Capture and Trial of Adolf Eichmann*)

The Holocaust also challenges blind faith in science and technology. The systematic extermination of thousands of people could not have taken place without the use of modern technology and the assistance of scientists. Engineers designed the extra-large crematoriums that were needed to dispose of the dead, just as they had earlier modified vehicles to channel the poisonous exhaust back inside the vans to gas the occupants. The death camps were run like modern factories, designed to mass-produce

Below: These gates lead to Belzec death camp in Poland, where around 500,000 Jews were gassed between March 1942 and May 1943.

corpses and dispose of them efficiently, and those controlling the camps sat in distant offices. As we now know, slaughter can be organized on a large scale without any blood getting on the hands of those responsible.

The Holocaust teaches us that many people, in many different ways, bear varying degrees of responsibility for what happened to 6 million Jews and members of other minority groups. We cannot point to one or two people and lay all the blame on them. There is not even the comfort that it could never happen again. Primo Levi, who survived life in Auschwitz, said "if the world could become convinced that Auschwitz never existed, it would be easier to build a second Auschwitz, and there is no assurance it would devour only Jews."

Below left: Young people visiting Auschwitz pass under the main gate and the words "Work Sets You Free." This slogan was put there by the SS when the camp first functioned as just a work camp.

Below right: Found guilty of attacking Nazi policies, Martin Niemöller was sent to Sachsenhausen and later Dachau concentration camps.

Then They Came For Me

Pastor Martin Niemöller was a Protestant minister who was twice arrested for attacking Nazi policies in Germany. He spent seven years in a concentration camp and wrote these memorable words after the war:

They came for the communists, and I wasn't a communist, so I didn't protest; They came for the socialists, and I wasn't a socialist, so I didn't protest; They came for the trade unionists but I wasn't a trade unionist, so I didn't protest; They came for the Jews, and I wasn't a Jew, so I didn't protest; Then they came for me, and there was no one left to protest.

TIMELINE

1915	Around 1.5 million Armenians die in Turkish genocide.
1917	Balfour Declaration promises a national home for Jews in Palestine.
1929–33	Genocide in Ukraine and other non-Russian regions of the USSR results in death of an estimated 12 million people.
1933–45	The Holocaust.
1939–45	World War II.
January 1945	Auschwitz death camp liberated by Soviet troops.
October 1945	Nuremberg trials begin in Germany.
1946	Anti-Semitic riot in Kielce, Poland.
1947	*Exodus* arrives in Palestine carrying illegal Jewish immigrants.
1948	State of Israel declared.
1960	Eichmann captured in Argentina and brought to Israel to face trial.
1975–79	Cambodian genocide, an estimated two million people die.
1987	Klaus Barbie, former head of the Gestapo in Lyon, faces trial in France.
1993	The United States Holocaust Memorial Museum opens in Washington, D.C. and the Simon Wiesenthal Center's Museum of Tolerance opens in Los Angeles.
1994	*Schindler's List* wins seven Oscars in Hollywood.
1999	Germany agrees to pay compensation to inmates of Nazi work camps; claims made for compensation against Swiss banks holding assets stolen from Jews during the Holocaust; claims made against Polish government for Jewish assets confiscated during and after the World War II.
2000	David Irving sues Deborah Lipstadt and Penguin Books for libel; permanent Holocaust exhibition opens at the Imperial War Museum in London and the Jewish Museum opens in Berlin.

RESOURCES

FURTHER READING AND SOURCES

Bauer, Yehuda. *History of the Holocaust*. Danbury, CT: Franklin Watts, 1992.

Dawidowicz, Lucy. *The War Against the Jews*. New York: Penguin, 1990.

Frank, Anne. *The Diary of Anne Frank*. New York: Bantam, 1993.

Friedlander, Saul. *Nazi Germany and the Jews: The Years of Persecution 1933-1939*. New York: HarperCollins, 1998.

Gilbert, Martin. *The Holocaust*. New York: Henry Holt, 1987.

Grant, R. G. *The Holocaust: New Perspectives*. New York: Raintree Steck-Vaughn, 1998.

Gutman, Israel. *Resistance: The Warsaw Ghetto Uprising*. New York: Houghton-Mifflin, 1997.

Hilberg, Raul. *The Destruction of the European Jews*. Holmes and Meier, 1985.

Keneally, Thomas. *Schindler's List*. Touchstone, 1993.

Laquer, Walter (ed). *The Holocaust Encyclopedia*. New Haven, CT: Yale University Press, 2001.

Levi, Primo. *Survival in Auschwitz*. New York: Simon and Schuster, 1996.

Rohrlich, Ruby (ed.) *Resisting the Holocaust*. New York: Berg, 1998.

Wiesel, Elie. *Night*. New York: Bantam, 1982.

INTERNET SITES

Shoah Visual History Foundation
www.vhf.org
Photographs and stories by survivors.

United States Holocaust Memorial Museum
www.ushmn.org
Pictorial history of the Holocaust

Yad Veshem
www.yad-vashem.org
Official website for the Holocaust Martyrs' and Heroes' Remembrance Authority

FILMS

The following movies are available for rent as videos or DVDs:

Schindler's List. Directed by Steven Spielberg from the book by Thomas Keneally, this is the story of a German factory owner who saved more than 1,000 Jews.

Shoah. Directed by Claude Lanzmann, this is a nine-hour documentary consisting entirely of interviews with survivors of and participants in the Holocaust.

Life is Beautiful. Directed by and starring Roberto Benigni, this controversial, Academy Award-winning film tells the fictional tale of an Italian Jewsih father who creates a kind of make-believe contest out of the Nazi occupation in order to shelter his son from the horrors of the Holocaust.

PLACES TO VISIT

United States Holocaust Memorial Museum
100 Raoul Wallenberg Place SW
Washington, D.C. 20024
Phone: (202) 488-0400
Website: www.ushm.org
Library: library@ushm.org
(202) 479-9717

GLOSSARY

Allies countries at war against Germany, Japan, and their allies.

anti-Semitism prejudice against Jews.

apartheid a system or policy of discriminating on the grounds of race.

Balfour Declaration a declaration made by the British Foreign Secretary, Lord Balfour, in 1917. It promised a national home for Jews in Palestine, while also promising to protect the rights of Arabs already living there.

Cold War a state of hostility between nations without actual fighting, used to describe relations between the U.S. and the USSR in the four decades after the end of the war in 1945.

collaborators people who cooperate traitorously with an enemy.

concentration camps large-scale prison and work camps, where prisoners were often worked to death but not in the systematic manner of the death camps.

death camps also known as extermination camps; designed to systematically murder their inmates, mostly Jews. The main Nazi death camps were in Poland: Auschwitz, Belzec, Chelmno, Majdanek, Sobibor, and Treblinka.

displaced persons (DP) a term for the millions of Europeans, both Jews and non-Jews, who found themselves without homes at the end of the World War II in 1945.

"ethnic cleansing" a polite expression for the compulsory expulsion, or murder, of communities because of their race or ethnicity.

Far Right a general term for right-wing, racist political groups that often express admiration for aspects of Hitler's Germany.

Final Solution phrase used by the Nazis when referring to the complete extermination of European Jews.

genocide the deliberate killing of a national, ethnic, racial, political, or religious group.

Gestapo the German secret police during the rule of the Nazis.

ghettos the poorest districts in some European towns, where Nazis forced Jews to live and from where they were transported to death camps.

Hippocratic Oath a sworn promise that doctors used to take about their obligations to their patients.

ideology the belief system or manner of thinking belonging to an individual or a group.

labor camps camps using slave labor, mostly prisoners of war and Jews, to increase Germany's wartime production.

laundering money distributing money that is likely to have been obtained illegally.

Palestine a much-disputed region in the eastern Mediterranean, currently part of Israel and Jordan.

psychopath someone whose mind and emotions are extremely unbalanced, making them aggressive and likely to commit violent crimes.

racism a belief in the superiority of a particular race.

SS (*Schutzstaffel*) in English "protection squads." Originally used as bodyguards to protect senior members of the Nazi Party, the SS developed into its most powerful organization and was responsible for controlling the concentration and death camps.

Untermenschen in English "subhuman." A Nazi term for certain ethnic groups, including Poles, Russians, and other Slavic people.

USSR abbreviation for the former Union of Soviet Socialist Republics, dominated by Russia, which broke up at the end of the 1980s.

Vatican the governing council, in Rome, of the Roman Catholic Church.

Zionism Jewish nationalist movement which aimed to found a Jewish national homeland in Palestine.

INDEX